MICHIGAN

Michigan, the state that got its name from the Indian word meaning "Great Lake," is truly a water wonderland. It touches on all but one of the Great Lakes and has 40,000 square miles of water within its boundaries.

Except for the region around Houghton, where the copper-bearing rocks have existed without change from the beginning of time, the land was formed by shallow seas and by glaciers. These last brought fertile soil from Canada.

Many different peoples lived in Michigan in prehistoric times. Burial mounds, implements, weapons, and 10,000 copper-mining pits tell of these early people.

Woodland Indians lived in the land when French explorers and fur traders first came to it.

The struggle between the French and English for Michigan ended only when the area became a part of the American *Northwest Territory*.

Once the timber, minerals, and fertile soil were discovered, settlers flocked to Michigan. They stayed to make this state first in production of automobiles, breakfast foods, furniture, sour cherries, cucumbers, navy beans, seedling pines.

The story of Michigan, like the story of America, is a dramatic one of the formation of the land and of the people who came to it and used it wisely. Its enchantment is in its beauty of woods and water and its limitless recreational facilities.

Enchantment of America

MICHIGAN

By Allan Carpenter

Illustrations by Phil Austin

CHILDRENS PRESS, Chicago

Regional Consultant for MICHIGAN
John Chavis
Curator Education Division
Detroit Historical Museum

For their advice and counsel and for the reference materials so generously furnished, I would like to express my appreciation to the following:

John Chavis, Curator Education Division, Detroit Historical Museum; Ruth Howard, Curator of Education, Kalamazoo Public Museum; Alexis A. Praus, Director, Kalamazoo Public Museum; Marion C. Forbes, Research Assistant, Dearborn Historical Museum; William C. Todd, Tourist and Convention Service, Henry Ford Museum and Greenfield Village; Michigan State Library, Lansing; Department of Public Instruction, Lynn B. Bartlett, Superintendent; Furniture Manufacturers Assn., Grand Rapids; Chamber of Commerce, Mackinac Island; Willard C. Wichers, Director, The Netherlands Museum, Holland; Ernest V. Blohm, Executive Secretary, Inter-Agency Council for Recreation; Lewis Beeson, Executive Secretary, Michigan Historical Commission; Henry J. Ponitz, Chief Adult Education, Department of Public Instruction, Lansing; Michigan Department of State; Robert J. Furlong, Director, State of Michigan Tourist Council; Dr. Arnold Pilling, Anthropologist, Wayne State University; Automotive Section, Detroit Public Library; Charles Hermann, Community Relations, Ford Motor Company; Richard Ruddell, Archivist, Ford Motor Company; Dr. Phillip Steinhaus, Carilloneur, Kirk-in-the-Hills; Frank L. DuMond, Director, Grand Rapids Public Museum.

Allan Carpenter

Contents

In the Name of the King!

A wooden cross lay on the bank of a river. Beside it was a cedar post, carrying a shield with the crest of King Louis the Fourteenth of France. Below rushed one of the mightiest rapids in the world. And all around for hundreds of miles stretched the wilderness.

Seated around the cross and the shield on the slope of the river bank was a great crowd of Indians from fourteen different tribes. They were not on the warpath. In fact, they were strangely silent, waiting for something to happen. For months they had been hearing about the wonderful things they would see on this day, the fourteenth of June, 1671. They were there at the invitation of their friends the French priests who had just built a mission near the rapids.

At last the door of the Mission opened, and a procession came out. Leading the procession were four missionaries in their black robes. Following them strode the most dramatic figure the Indians had ever seen, wearing his most beautiful uniform as an officer of the French King. After him came his attendants, interpreters, and many French hunters and trappers, all wearing bright-colored sashes and anything else they might have to make them look more impressive to the Indians.

The solemn procession halted before the cross. As it was being planted in the ground, the great cross was blessed. Next the pole with the shield was raised with a chant and a prayer for the King. The officer stepped forward while guns were fired, drew his sword and slashed a piece of sod from the earth. Holding the sod aloft in one hand and his sword raised in the other, in a loud voice he claimed for his King all the land to the ocean of the North, to the ocean of the West and to the ocean of the South. He repeated this three times, while his followers shouted, "Long live the King!" and fired their muskets.

The officer was Francois Daumont, who is generally known by his title "Sieur de St. Lusson." He had been sent by the Governor of Canada to make a formal claim to most of the North American continent in the name of the King of France. To make the act seem even more official, St. Lusson asked the priests and other white men to witness and sign a report that the land was now officially French.

One of the missionaries, Father Allouez, next made a speech about the power of the King. "When he attacks, he is more terrible than the thunder; the air and the sea are set on fire by the discharges of his cannon. . . ." At the end of the speech the Indians shouted in amazement. They "were all astonished to hear that there was any man on earth so great, rich, and powerful."

The Indians could not know then that they had just seen the start of the events which would lead to the loss of their beloved hunting grounds.

This is only one of the many stories of enchantment of Michigan, as it took place on the banks of the St. Marys River where Sault Ste. Marie stands today.

Lay of the Land

Water Wonderland

Many people fear that some day there will not be enough fresh water to go around, and many states and cities will begin to suffer for lack of water. If that day ever comes, Michigan will be the most favored state of all. For Michigan really is, as its slogan goes, a "Water Wonderland."

In the Indian language "Michi" means great or large. "Gama" is the word for lake. So the name of Michigan itself comes from the Indian word meaning "Great Lake." Michigan can truly claim to be the land of the great lakes, since no other state touches all but one of the Great Lakes. Only Lake Ontario fails to wash the shores of the state of Michigan. So important have the lakes been in Michigan's history that the state has been called the "Child of the Great Lakes."

The lakes come between the upper and the lower parts of Michigan, making it the only state on the continent that has two parts completely separated from one another in such a way.

Michigan is the largest state east of the Mississippi River, but it holds this record only because of its great amount of water. The land area of Michigan is 57,022 square miles. Other eastern states are larger than this, but add almost 40,000 square miles of water within Michigan's Great Lakes boundaries and Michigan becomes the largest eastern state. Michigan includes four times as much water-covered area as any other state.

The two square miles of water for every three square miles of land give Michigan the greatest proportion of fresh water to land of any similar area in the world.

It seems strange indeed that an inland state, far from any ocean coast, should have more shoreline than any of the states with long ocean coastlines, but Michigan once had the longest shoreline of all the states. It was only when Alaska became a state that Michigan's coastline of 3,121 miles lost its first-place rank and dropped to second.

In addition to the Great Lakes, Michigan has 11,000 inland lakes, many of them of good size. No place in Michigan is more than eighty-

five miles from a Great Lake or more than a few minutes by automobile from some lake.

The four Great Lakes surrounding Michigan also help to make the climate warmer in winter and cooler in summer than it would be otherwise.

Michigan also has many rivers. The Detroit River, the St. Marys River, and the St. Clair River are among the most important waterways in the world, connecting the three upper Great Lakes with the St. Lawrence River and finally with the seven seas. Some of the other Michigan rivers are the Rouge, Saginaw, Grand, Black, and St. Joseph.

There are many things about the geography of Michigan that seem strange. Port Huron in Michigan is as far east as Greenville, South Carolina. Ironwood, Michigan, is farther west than St. Louis, Missouri. It is farther from Detroit to Houghton, still in the state of Michigan, than it is from Detroit to Baltimore in the "far-off" state of Maryland.

Britain, Sweden, and Belgium are closer to Detroit by water than is New York City. And, strangely enough, a portion of Canada lies to the south of Michigan, although we think of Canada as our neighbor to the north.

Before the Memory of Man

Michigan was not always like it is today. Both sandstone and limestone are found in Michigan. Sandstone comes from the packed sand of ancient beaches around ancient seas. Limestone comes from the crushing and packing together of the shells of dead animals of the

ocean. Because sandstone and limestone are found where oceans have once been, experts in geology believe that Michigan must have been at the bottom of a shallow ocean at one time, and possibly several times, as the oceans came and went millions of years ago.

Much later Michigan was almost entirely covered by water again, but this time it was the frozen water of the glaciers during the ice ages. Several times the sheets of ice pushed over what is now Michigan, bringing with them rich soil from Canada, great rocks and boulders, and as the ice melted, leaving behind them valleys and hollow places they had carved out of the land. Many of these hollow places became lakes. Even the Great Lakes were formed in this way.

A few areas still to be seen in Michigan today were not changed by the seas or glaciers. One of the most interesting places anywhere is the region near Houghton. The copper-bearing rocks there are believed to be among the oldest rock formations in all the world, apparently having existed there practically without change almost from the beginning of time.

Collecting Your Thoughts

Would you agree that Michigan is a "Water Wonderland?" Why?

Trace the whole of Michigan's coastline on a map, both upper and lower peninsulas.

What are some of the most interesting "records" Michigan holds because of her land and its geography?

What were the most important forces that operated to change Michigan in ancient days?

Footsteps on the Land

They Never Were Seen

Before the white man came to Michigan, there were no written records of the people who lived there. However, we know there were many different people who occupied the region we call Michigan today. They left various kinds of indications that tell us something about them and the way they lived, but we really know very little about them. We have found a few of the mounds they made as burial places for their dead or for other purposes. Some of their ancient implements and weapons have been discovered.

Not as many of these reminders of ancient peoples are found in Michigan as in some of the nearby states. Some of the most interesting traces left by prehistoric man are found on Isle Royale. There have been found 10,000 copper mining pits worked by prehistoric peoples. We can only guess from this that some early Americans were skilled enough to work with copper at about the same time the ancient people of Egypt and the Sudan began to fashion the metal in their desert land so far away from Michigan.

By the time white men had arrived in Michigan territory, the Indians they found there were different from those who were expert enough to work copper. For some reason the native people of Michigan were still in the primitive stone age.

Makers of Snowshoes and Builders of Canoes

When the white man came to what is now Michigan, he found Chippewa (sometimes called Ojibway), Ottawa, Potowatomi, Miami, and Menominee Indian tribes living in various parts of Michigan. Later the Wyandot (or Huron) group came. Wars and changing food supply kept the Indians on the move, so that the various tribes occupied many different areas at different times in history.

The fierce Iroquois Indians had driven almost all the other Indians out of the lower peninsula of Michigan, and for years this was practically a "no man's land." When the white men came, they also avoided the Iroquois, and the first settlements were in the far-off upper peninsula, as far away from the Iroquois as possible.

Although they were backward, the Indians made two great contributions to the white man. Without the Indians' snowshoes, it was impossible to travel overland in the heavy Michigan snows, and their bark canoes have been called the "cleverest small craft ever devised by man."

The Indians hated their enemies, but although they were much misunderstood by the white men, they were loyal to their friends. It was the coming of the whites that caused their downfall.

Under Four Flags

The first white men to reach what is now Michigan came from the older French settlements along the St. Lawrence River. They were still looking for a way to cross the American continent and reach the Pacific Ocean where they thought they would find the Orient and all its riches. It is generally agreed that Etienne Brule and his companion, Grenoble, were the first white men to touch Michigan soil. They are supposed to have reached Michigan sometime between 1618 and 1622, and at about the same time they discovered the largest of the Great Lakes—Lake Superior.

Another young French explorer who was searching for China was Jean Nicolet. The Governor of Canada was so sure Nicolet would reach China that he gave him a beautiful silk robe, decorated with

heavy gold braid and jewels so that he would be suitably dressed to meet the Emperor of China. Nicolet probably made his way through the Straits of Mackinac and may have reached as far into the interior as Green Bay in Wisconsin. Although his gorgeous robes were very impressive to the Indians, he was disappointed in not reaching the Orient.

Other French explorers, fur traders, and missionaries began to reach the upper Michigan country. Two Jesuit missionaries, Fathers Jogues and Raymbault gave the name Sault de Sainte Marie to the rapids in the river that flows between Lakes Superior and Huron, and it has been the region of the Sault (or Soo) ever since.

The very first permanent white settlement not only in Michigan but in all the Midwest was made there. The settlement at the Soo was founded in 1668 by the famous Jesuit missionary Father Jacques Marquette and his companion Father Claude Dablon. It was here three years later that the Pageant of the Sault took place, with France claiming most of North America as her own territory.

Although the white man had been in upper Michigan for many years, it was not until 1669 that any white person visited the Lower Peninsula. Adrien Jolliet, older brother of the famous explorer Louis Jolliet, is supposed to have been the first white man to go into the lower part of Michigan.

Most of the French in Michigan were fur traders and missionaries. Some of these expert French woodsmen were called *coureurs de bois*, and others *voyageurs*, or boatmen. The traders were successful in buying great quantities of valuable furs from the Indians, and the missionaries appeared to be successful in converting a number of the Indians to Christianity.

But not many Frenchmen came as settlers to occupy and farm the new lands. In 1689 there were only 20,000 people in all of the French colonies of North America. Although most of the English settlers were found along the Atlantic Coast, in that year there were already more than 300,000 English settlers in North America.

Alarmed at the growing power of the British, the French began to build forts. In 1679 the famous French explorer La Salle built the first French fort in Michigan on the site of what is now St. Joseph, and called it Fort Miami. This became a thriving military and trading post.

In order to transport his furs to market, La Salle built the first large sailing boat to sail on the Great Lakes and called it the "Griffon."

Loaded with furs, the "Griffon" set sail one day in 1679 and was never heard of again. What happened to the "Griffon" and its cargo and crew is one of the real mysteries of the Great Lakes.

By 1700 the French were more disturbed than ever about the British, who were competing for the fur trade in territories the French claimed as their own. In 1701 a French officer founded a town on the river between Lake Huron and Lake Erie, at a spot where the river runs through a narrow strait. So he called it by the French word for "The Strait"—Detroit. Detroit is the oldest of all the major cities of the Midwest.

One of the famous names in America is that of the French officer who founded Detroit. But most people know his name not because of his success in establishing a great American city but because in that same city more than 200 years later a group of men gave his name to an automobile. Today we see the name of the founder of Detroit, Antoine de la Mothe Cadillac, on most streets in the United States.

Soon Madame Cadillac and the wife of Cadillac's assistant, Madame Tonty, made the long and hard journey to join their husbands in Detroit. They became the first white women in Michigan. Cadillac had brought 150 persons to Detroit and by his firm and fair treatment he gained the respect of the Indians.

Because many French leaders were afraid of his power and were jealous of him, Cadillac at last was forced to leave Detroit in 1711, but he was given an even higher post, that of governor of far-away Louisiana.

Still disturbed by the threat of the British, the French set up Fort Michilimackinac on the Straits of Mackinac in 1715.

During the years that followed, the French and the British were sometimes at war, sometimes at peace. At last, however, in the war we call the French and Indian War the British were successful. Major Robert Rogers and 200 of his Royal English Rangers occupied Detroit in 1760, without a struggle. French rule of Michigan was almost at an end.

The French settlers accepted the British rule without much complaint, but before long the English were having many difficulties with the Indians. The French had treated the Indians as their friends. They often invited them to be guests in their homes, and many marriages of French men and Indian women took place.

The British, however, considered the Indians inferior, and generally treated them with little regard.

A famous Indian Chief, Pontiac, resented the British and decided to organize a movement to drive them out. He planned to capture Detroit by a trick. He had the barrels of his guns filed off so they could be carried under the blankets the Indians wore. He asked to speak to the British commander at Detroit and brought his warriors into the fort with their concealed weapons, but the commander, Major Glad-

win, had been warned, and he had so many soldiers armed and ready that Pontiac decided against trying to carry out his plan.

Later, in 1763, he attacked the fort at Detroit and began the longest siege in the history of Indian warfare. For 175 days the Indians tried to capture Detroit. At the beginning Major Gladwin had only 100 soldiers and 20 merchants to hold off the hundreds of Indians, but Pontiac was never able to take Detroit.

Detroit, however, was the only fort in Michigan that did not fall to the Indians.

19

The Indians planned another trick to capture the fort at Mackinac City. This time they were successful. The Indians started to play a game of lacrosse outside the fort. The British soldiers came outside to watch, leaving the gates open. They paid little attention to the squaws who strolled inside the fort, but the squaws carried knives and other arms under their blankets. On a signal, the Indians left their game, hurried into the fort where they received arms from the squaws already inside, and then massacred the defenders.

This was the period of the Indian's greatest success in his struggle with the white men.

In spite of his victories, Pontiac finally was forced to make peace, and the British again gained control of Michigan.

But their control was not to go unchallenged for very long. The Americans began their revolution against Britain in 1776. Very little effect of the Revolution was felt in Michigan. The British commander at Detroit, Lietuenant Governor Henry Hamilton, became one of the most hated men in American history for his part in the American Revolution.

Hamilton was called the "Hair Buyer," because he offered the Indians money for American scalps. He felt this would help to destroy American settlements.

During the Revolution, in 1781, one of the strange happenings in Michigan history was the raid of a Spanish party from the Spanish lands west of the Mississippi. The raiding party reached the fort at Niles, which they captured and held for several days. This was the only spot in Michigan where the Spanish flag ever flew, but it can be truthfully said that four flags have flown over Michigan—French, British, Spanish and American.

American or Not, That Is the Question

When the Revolution was over in America, the Treaty of Paris in 1783 gave Michigan to the Americans. In spite of this, the British kept their control in Michigan for another thirteen years, and the Americans were not strong enough to do anything about it. The British were determined to protect their rich fur trade in the region as long as possible.

After many defeats by the Indians, who were receiving much help and encouragement from the British, the Americans finally sent a famous Revolutionary War hero to capture the western lands. This was General Anthony Wayne, who was called "Mad Anthony Wayne" because he took such "mad" risks during the Revolution.

With very brilliant and careful planning and preparation, General Wayne was successful, and the Jay Treaty of 1794 finally gave the United States the right to occupy her lands in Michigan.

General Wayne himself traveled to Detroit in August, 1796, and the whole town turned out to welcome him on one of the most joyful celebrations the city has ever known. The name of "The Chief Who Never Sleeps," as the Indians called him, has been given to a city, a county, a university, a fort, and a museum—all in Michigan and all named "Wayne."

Today, with the exception of some names and memories, there is very little remaining of the long rule of the French and the shorter rule of the British in Michigan.

Even before Michigan came under American rule, the young mother country had set up plans for governing it. The Northwest Ordinance of 1787 established the Northwest Territory, which now includes the states of Ohio, Indiana, Illinois, Wisconsin, part of Minnesota, and Michigan.

The Northwest Ordinance was one of the great laws of history. It set the whole pattern for the growth of the United States. Instead of having the western lands governed as colonies, they were to be given the opportunity to become states with all the privileges of the original thirteen states. If some other plan had been tried in the Northwest Territory, the United States might have been quite different.

Michigan remained a part of the Northwest Territory until 1800, when it was placed in what was known as Indiana Territory. In 1805, Michigan became a separate territory, with Detroit as its capital, although not all of present-day Michigan was included in this territory.

At last, after almost 150 years, the people of Michigan were going to have at least a small voice in their own government. President Thomas Jefferson appointed William Hull the new territorial governor, Stanley Griswold, secretary, and Samuel Huntington, Augustus Woodward, and Frederick Bates judges.

Their new capital, Detroit, was still only a small trading town, although it had been in existence for over 100 years and had been incorporated in 1802.

Before the new governor could reach his capital, a fire broke out in John Harvey's stable. The great fire of 1805 spread; people left their homes; before evening almost all of Detroit's buildings lay in a heap of wood ashes, through which ruined and smoking chimneys reached toward the sky.

It was only about two weeks after the fire that Governor Hull arrived for the first time, to find his new capital nothing but a ruined heap. Father Gabriel Richard of Detroit, who then was the only clergyman in all of Michigan, surveyed the ruins of the city he loved and said, "We hope for better things; it will arise from its ashes." His words have been used in the present seal of the city of Detroit.

When Judge Woodward arrived, he agreed with Father Richard that this great tragedy might lead to something better. He drew up elaborate plans for a very large and beautiful city, based on the plans of the national Capital, Washington, D. C. Although the city never followed the plan to any great extent, some of Detroit is still laid out in the way that Judge Woodward intended. The United States Congress gave Detroit 10,000 acres of land which could be sold for funds to rebuild the city. Gradually, indeed, the city was rebuilt.

During the early 1800's Michigan did not experience much growth, although new undertakings were going forward. John Jacob Astor established his American Fur Company headquarters at Mackinac Island in 1808, and this was one of the sources of his great wealth.

By this time, the Indians were growing restless again. America was having constant and increasing trouble with Great Britain, and the English never lost an opportunity to stir up the Indians against the Americans.

In 1812 the trouble between Britain and America turned into a war. Michigan Territory was not ready for war, nor was the rest of the country. Governor Hull, who had been a fine general in the Revolutionary War, was asked to take the military command at Detroit. He refused because he felt that Detroit could not be protected as long as the British controlled Lake Erie, but he finally changed his mind and took the command.

Before the war had gone on very long, General Hull surrendered Detroit to the British without a fight. Fort Mackinac had already fallen. His reasons for surrendering were disputed, and the American people were bitter about this defeat. General Hull was court martialed and found guilty of neglect of duty and unofficerlike conduct. He received the death sentence, which later was remitted by President Madison.

Once again, Michigan was in the hands of the British.

British Colonel Henry Proctor was sent to take charge at Detroit. This was a very difficult time for the people of the city. The Indians of the neighborhood gave Detroiters a particularly bad time, stealing and tormenting as much as they could. They even stole the pipes of Father Richard's organ. But the priest managed to get the word to the Indians that this was the flute of the Great Spirit. The Indians wanted nothing to do with such powerful magic, so one night the pipes were replaced in the organ as mysteriously as they had disappeared.

It was not until Commodore Perry's great victory over the British navy on Lake Erie in 1813 that it was possible for American forces to retake Detroit. General Proctor burned the public buildings of Detroit and left the city. Two days later, in September, 1813, General Duncan McArthur brought Detroit back under American control, to the joy of the inhabitants.

The war ended officially with the Treaty of Ghent. Both sides agreed to give up all territories they had conquered and return to the boundaries as they were before the war.

In order to help return good feelings on both sides, the leading citizens of Detroit gave a dinner party on March 29, 1815. They called this a "Pacification Dinner," and they invited many British and Canadian people from across the border. This act of good will did much to restore the pleasant relations of the people of Michigan with their Canadian neighbors.

Since the War of 1812, there has been little need for defenses on the border between Canada and the United States.

A State or Not, That Is the Question

Lewis Cass was made governor of the Michigan territory in October of 1813. Someone has said that "Detroit's real history began with the appointment of Lewis Cass as the civil administrator of the territory."

The war had left the people of Michigan, and especially of Detroit, in great want. The government had to bring in food and supplies as quickly as possible.

A government surveyor had reported that most of the land in Michigan was practically worthless, "interminable swamp, miserably poor." Those Americans who wanted government lands looked elsewhere for many years after this report came out in 1815.

Governor Cass was determined to give his territory a better name. After the territory was enlarged in 1818 to include part of present-day Wisconsin and parts of present upper Michigan, the governor decided to explore his territories. In 1820 he and his party started their long journey.

At the Sault, he found the Indians angry. One of the chiefs even raised a British flag. Governor Cass hurried over to the flag and tore it down, saying he would not permit a foreign flag on American soil. For a time it appeared the Indians might go on the warpath, but they kept the peace. The Governor's bravery was one of the reasons for this.

Governor Cass had with him on the trip a number of experts, including Henry R. Schoolcraft, a geologist. Schoolcraft found many valuable minerals on the journey and the report of the trip caused people to change their minds about Michigan. The Governor and his party went on to the Mississippi and traveled up the river for 350 miles, hoping to find the source, but the coming winter made them turn back. They had made a difficult journey of over 4,000 miles, principally by canoe, without losing a man.

Another important event in Michigan history at this time was the coming of the first steamboat. This was the "Walk-in-the-Water." When it first came to Detroit, the Indians stared in amazement at this wonderful ship that sailed along majestically without either oars or sails. As a joke, they were told that the reason the boat moved was that a whole school of sturgeon had been put into harnesses, and these fish were pulling the boat through the water, swimming below the surface where they could not be seen.

Within a surprisingly short time, many other steamboats had been built, and passengers and freight were moving between Buffalo and Detroit and other Michigan areas on regular schedules. Then in 1825 the Erie Canal opened, making an easy water route clear across New York State. This meant that people from New England and every other part of the East could come to Michigan by water much more easily than they could reach other western lands, and they could bring more of the necessities of life with them by boat than they could by any overland route.

This advantage attracted settlers to Michigan country, and large numbers began to arrive in the territory. Michigan was beginning to take advantage of her Water Wonderland.

In 1828 the territorial capitol building at Detroit was completed. Travelers came from miles around to see this structure, which towered over the other buildings of Detroit to the amazing height of 140 feet.

Then in 1831 occurred one of the most unusual events in American history. President Andrew Jackson appointed Stevens T. Mason secretary of the Michigan Territory. The territorial governor at that time, George B. Porter, was often away from Michigan, which made Secretary Mason the acting governor and the leader of the territory. This would not seem strange except for the fact that Stevens T. Mason was only nineteen years old when he first became acting governor. He is thought to be the youngest man ever to serve in such a post in the United States.

The people of Michigan were greatly upset. They felt that a boy had no business in such a high office, but the boy governor quickly convinced both the President and his fellow citizens that even though he was too young to vote, he could manage government affairs with skill. He promised always to listen to the counsel of older and more experienced men. In 1834, Governor Porter died, and Mason continued on as acting governor. Michigan, as a territory, never had another governor.

In 1832, the Indian Chief, Black Hawk, stirred up difficulties between his people and the whites, and Michigan armed for war. There was no fighting in Michigan during the Black Hawk War, but for a while most of the people were afraid it might come.

After Black Hawk had been defeated and had made peace with the government, he was taken on a tour of the East to impress him with the white man's power. On his return to the West, in July of 1833, he passed through Detroit. The whole town turned out to celebrate the Fourth of July by seeing this famous warrior.

The dignified old chief wore a long blue coat and spectacles; his head was covered with a magnificent snow-white top hat, and he carried a handsome cane. He paid a courtesy call on Acting Governor Mason. He was scarcely the savage that many people might have expected.

Although the Black Hawk rebellion brought no battles to Michigan soil, it did bring another tragedy. A steamer with soldiers on board docked at Detroit, and before it was discovered that there was serious illness on board, numerous Detroit people were infected. An epidemic of the feared disease of cholera was started. Many died, and the doctors were not able to keep up with the needs for medical attention.

Father Gabriel Richard "might be seen clothed in the robes of his high calling, pale and emaciated, with spectacles on his forehead and prayer book in his hand, going from house to house to visit his parishioners, encouraging the well, and administering spiritual consolation to the sick and dying." The disease had almost run its course when Father Richard became infected himself, and the priest, who has been called one of Michigan's greatest citizens, died on September 13, 1832. He had worn himself out with his years of labor for his adopted state and with work for his people, particularly during the awful months of the cholera epidemic.

His funeral was attended by more than two thousand people, a crowd larger than the whole population of the city of Detroit at that time.

"From early morn until dark the church was filled with the multitude who had come from all quarters to take a last glimpse of him. His remains were followed to the grave amid the solemn tolling of all the bells of the city, and followed by a large concourse of citizens of all classes and denominations who evinced the deepest sorrow . . ."

With the threat of Indian troubles in the past, and government land available at low prices, more and more people began to come to Michigan. One of the visitors, Mrs. Annie B. Jameson, gives an interesting picture of the Michigan frontier in those days of the 1830's:

"The spires and towers of the city of Detroit were seen against the western sky. The schooners at anchor, or dropping into the river—

the little canoes flitting across from side to side—the lofty buildings—the enormous steamers—the noisy port, and busy streets, all bathed in the light of a sunset such as I had never seen, not even in Italy—almost turned me giddy with excitement . . ."

Mrs. Jameson also describes a party of immigrants from Vermont who were headed west. "They have two wagons covered with canvas, a yoke of oxen, and a pair of horses . . . The father is an old Vermont farmer . . . He has with him fifteen children of different ages . . . all are barefoot except the two eldest girls who are uncommonly handsome with fine dark eyes."

One of the pleasures of the people of Detroit in those days was riding back and forth on the ferry to Canada. As Mrs. Jameson described it, "English emigrants and French Canadians; brisk Americans; dark, sad-looking Indians folded in their blankets; farmers, store-keepers . . . over-dressed, long waisted damsels, attended by their beaux."

During the years between 1807 and 1842 the Indians agreed to many treaties, giving up their lands in Michigan. As more land became available and as the value of the forests and minerals became better known, it appeared that everyone wanted to go to Michigan. In the ten years between 1830 and 1840 so many people caught "Michigan fever" that the population increased from 31,000 to 212,000.

By 1835 Michigan qualified to become a state. In that year the people of Michigan adopted a state government and elected officers. Stevens T. Mason, who had then reached only twenty-four years of age, was elected the first governor of the state of Michigan, but the United States Congress refused to recognize the new state. This was the only time in the history of the United States when a state government was actually operating over a period of years while the state was not officially admitted to the Union, and while the territorial government was continuing to operate at the same time.

One of the problems that kept Michigan away from statehood was the quarrel with Ohio concerning the southern boundary. Both Michigan and Ohio claimed an area west of Lake Erie which includes the city of Toledo. Some misunderstandings had created doubt as to exactly where the boundary had been intended to be. For a while it looked as if the two states would actually go to war to support their claims.

In the end, Michigan gave up the disputed land and accepted the whole western portion of the upper peninsula to make up for it. There were many who thought this was a poor bargain for Michigan, but it was not long before the great mineral wealth of the peninsula area became known, and it appeared that Michigan had gained a great deal by "losing" the "border war" with Ohio.

With the settlement of the boundary dispute, Congress was ready to consider Michigan's bid to become a state. Statehood had been delayed for yet another reason. Those who wanted to keep slavery or to enlarge the areas where it was permitted did not want to see Michigan become a state, since it would be a free state, without slavery.

But in 1836, Arkansas was admitted as a slave state so Congress decided to pair it with a free state. This was done, and Michigan was admitted to full statehood in January, 1837, becoming the twenty-sixth state in the Union.

After so many years as governor in everything but name, Stevens T. Mason took over as governor in actual fact. The two senators and one representative elected by Michigan, who had been trying to get into Congress since 1835, finally were permitted to take their seats.

Collecting Your Thoughts

Name three occasions when there were difficulties between the Indians and the white men in Michigan. What caused these difficulties?

Find traces of the French and British influence that still remain in Michigan today.

List three effects of the Black Hawk War in Michigan.

Tell a number of reasons why the population of Michigan grew so rapidly in the years between 1825 and 1840.

Why do many people think the settlement of the "border war" with Ohio resulted in an advantage for Michigan?

Yesterday and Today

Of Governors, Kings and Capitals

The year 1837 was not a very good year for a new state. In fact, it was not a very good year for any state. The country had begun to suffer a depression, and Michigan was especially hard hit. Many banks failed. There was little money to be used. The state owed five million dollars. Work on canals, railroads and other public improvements had almost been halted.

To add to the problems, a strange series of events took place in Michigan in 1838. A group of people in Canada wanted to overthrow the British and have a free Canada. They had many supporters in the United States. These supporters held a mass meeting at Detroit, broke into the Detroit jail and stole arms and ammunition, then seized the schooner Ann. They were all ready to attack Canada.

Several times the American friends of the Canadians attempted to go to the aid of their friends in Canada but each time they were kept back, until December of 1838, when an American group managed to land above Windsor. They were soon killed or captured.

Governor Mason had a difficult time. He sympathized with the Americans who wanted to help the Canadian rebels, but he was forced to try to keep them in check. United States officials could not permit their people to attack a friendly government.

After two years as governor, the "boy governor" said he would not run for another term, and William Woodbridge was elected as the second governor of Michigan. He had been a prominent figure in Michigan history since early territorial days.

Another prominent early Michigan man made an extremely important discovery in 1840. Dr. Douglass Houghton, who was the state geologist, had found important copper deposits in the upper peninsula. It had always been thought that large amounts of copper might be found there, but Dr. Houghton's discoveries provided accurate proof of this by a scientist. These discoveries were to influence Michigan's future more than almost anything else that had happened before.

Only five years later, Dr. Houghton lost his life in a storm on Lake Superior while he was on another voyage of discovery.

A peculiar chapter of Michigan history took place on Beaver Island at about this time. A group of members of the Church of Jesus Christ of Latter Day Saints had settled on the island in 1846.

Their leader on Beaver Island was James Jesse Strang. Strang had himself proclaimed King of the Island. "King Strang" ruled his followers with an iron hand, maintaining an absolute monarchy in his island domain. This was the first and only time in United States history that such a thing has taken place.

Because these Mormons, as the Latter Day Saints are called, appeared to be different from most people, they had a difficult time wherever they went. This was especially true when they had a "king" among democratic Americans. Feelings finally grew so high that there was a "battle" in 1854 between the Mormon settlers and Irish settlers.

In 1856, Strang was assassinated. Mobs from the mainland forced the Mormons off the island and took their property. Today there remain only a few memories of King James the First.

Just a year after the Mormons settled on Beaver Island, another group of settlers came to Michigan. These were the Dutch, refugees from religious persecution in Holland, who founded the town of Holland in Michigan in 1847. After many hard times and disasters, the hard-working Dutch settlers finally became successful in their community, and they remain so today.

Until this time Detroit had remained not only the principal city but the capital of Michigan. Now, however, the state legislature was determined to move the capital to another location, but so many of the lawmakers had their own favorite cities it was impossible to select one.

BEAVER ISLAND

Finally, they decided they would have to select a location that was not connected with any of them, and in 1847 Lansing was chosen to be the new capital. People could hardly believe that their new capital was to be in the heart of a woodland wilderness where there was only one log house and a sawmill. The new capital had no roads, and could only be reached by an Indian trail.

Nevertheless, the capital was moved to Lansing in January of 1848 and became the "capital in the forest." The first Capitol building was made of the wonderful walnut trees from the nearby woodlands.

Freedom For All?

By this time the people of Michigan were concerned with a problem that was every day more widely splitting the people of the United States. This was the problem of slavery.

The abolitionists, who wanted to "abolish" slavery, were strong in Michigan. Many Michigan people helped slaves to escape to Canada

over the system of hideouts that was given the name "Underground Railroad."

Those who were opposed to slavery were dissatisfied with the old political parties. In 1854 a group of anti-slavery people called a meeting at Jackson, Michigan, to establish a new political party in which they felt they could have confidence.

So many people came to Jackson that there was no building large enough to hold the crowd. They met outdoors in what has been called the "Convention Under the Oaks," and chose the name Republican for their party. Several states claim to have been the birthplace of the national Republican party. Among these, Michigan has one of the strongest claims because of the convention at Jackson on July 6, 1854.

Michigan has an even firmer position in the beginning of the Republican party because of the election of 1854. Michigan's Republicans won the election, and Michigan was the first state to have a Republican Governor, Kingsley Bingham. The Republicans also won three of the four seats in the United States House of Representatives, as well as both houses of the state legislature.

Neither Republicans nor Democrats could keep the arguments over slavery from becoming stronger as the years went by. At last the horrors of civil war came to a country that was not prepared for it.

During the first year of fighting, twenty-one Michigan regiments were formed. Michigan men fought in most of the early battles of the war in the East, when most people thought the war would be over in a few months at the most.

As the war went on, Michigan soldiers gained a reputation for their courage. Among the most heroic of these were the men of the Michigan Cavalry Brigade led by General George Armstrong Custer. This brigade played a key part in the Confederate defeat at Gettysburg.

Soldiers of the Michigan Engineers and Mechanics took an important part in another prominent operation of the war. The Union troops in Chattanooga were surrounded by Confederates and would have starved for lack of supplies. Just in time the Union armies were able to build a road and a pontoon bridge to reach their forces in Chattanooga. The Michigan Engineers placed the bridge in position over the Tennessee River, and it was given the name "Michigan Bridge."

In helping to take Missionary Ridge near Chattanooga, the 11th Michigan Infantry performed one of the most spectacular charges of the whole war.

A brave Michigan boy, Charles Howard Gardner, entered the Civil War service at the age of twelve to keep from being separated from his teacher.

Even a few women managed to fight in the Civil War. The most famous female soldier from Michigan was Sarah Emma Edmonds. She enlisted as Franklin Thompson and concealed her identity for two years. She fought with the Second Michigan Infantry in four major campaigns, and as a spy narrowly escaped with her life several times. Her most successful "disguise" as a spy was that of a woman.

At the end of the war, the Fourth Michigan Cavalry became one of the most famous outfits in either army by carrying out the outstanding capture of the war. They discovered a camp where Jefferson Davis, the President of the Southern Confederacy, was hiding, took him prisoner, and brought their noted captive to Federal authorities.

A total of 92,000 Michigan men had served in the Civil War—a very large percentage of a state with such a small population as Michigan then had. Fourteen thousand Michigan men lost their lives in battle and 10,000 more died of disease. Many Michigan men received the nation's highest honor, the Congressional Medal of Honor, but two men from Michigan received it twice. These were Thomas W. Custer, brother of General George Custer, and Frank D. Baldwin.

Although most people know of the great Chicago fire which began on October 8, 1871, very few people know that on the same day a great fire swept across Michigan, killing more people than the Chicago fire. The strong winds united several Michigan brush fires, and swept rapidly through the Michigan timber. Holland, Michigan, was destroyed just as it was preparing to celebrate its twenty-fifth anniversary. Manistee was partially destroyed, and the fire swept clear across the state. Eighteen thousand Michigan people were left without homes.

It is strange to think that while fire was devouring so much of the Michigan forests, at the very same time fire was destroying the wooden buildings of Chicago, which had been built almost entirely of the white pine from the Michigan woodlands.

Ten years later, another Michigan forest fire killed 125 people and swept across a very large area.

Michigan was one of the first states in which organizations sprang up to help the laboring people. The state has long been known as a center for the formation and growth of labor unions. In 1885, Michigan labor won one of its greatest victories with the passage of a law declaring ten hours as a legal day's work.

In 1897, Hazen Pingree, one of the state's most popular politicians, became governor of Michigan. When he was elected governor, he was also mayor of Detroit. He kept both of those positions until the state Supreme Court ruled that he could retain only one post, so he resigned as mayor.

During this same period, several Michigan men became interested in a new activity that was to change the whole course of life for

Michigan and its people, as well as the world at large. This was the automobile industry, which will be covered in detail in a later section.

The war known to us as the First World War began in Europe in 1914. Although America did not actually enter the war against Germany until 1917, Detroit became the center of much German spy activity. When the United States did come into the war, the men of the 32nd division became the first American troops on German soil, although this did not take place until the war was nearing its end. The 32nd contained one of the largest groups of Michigan soldiers in any division.

After the war, changes came quickly. William B. Stout produced America's first all-metal airplane. This later developed into the famous Ford trimoter airplane, which was a great influence in developing the commercial airlines so common today. It can truly be said that Michigan has played a key part in both the automobile and aviation industries.

Some of the old Ford trimotors are still flying cargoes today after almost forty years. The nation's first regularly scheduled airline passenger service was begun in Michigan in 1926, between Detroit and Grand Rapids.

The great depression of 1929 had a worse effect on Michigan than on many other states, because so many people depended on industry in Michigan. Few people had money to buy automobiles and the other major products of Michigan, so that unemployment was particularly serious.

The country was not yet over the effects of the depression when another war began—a war which was to be the worst the world had ever known.

An enormous total of 673,000 Michigan men and women served in the U.S. armed forces during the World War II. The Red Arrow division, which included a large percentage of Michigan men, was one of the first American groups to meet the Japanese in the South Pacific. The Red Arrow's combat record of 654 days has never been equalled.

During the war, the Soo area was the most heavily guarded spot in the United States. If the enemy had been able to destroy the locks there, they might have crippled a large part of the country's war manufacturing.

In World War II, the war plants of Michigan produced the unbelievable total of one-eighth of all the war material produced in the whole United States. This record far surpassed that of any other state. For the war, Michigan produced a total of twenty-seven billion dollars worth of war munitions.

The Willow Run plant of Ford could build a B 24 bomber every hour. The Defoe Company became the region's largest producer of fighting boats. They developed a new method of production permitting them to turn out a complete boat every week.

Even Michigan children did their part. Michigan's young people contributed the money that purchased a glider. This glider happened to be the first glider to land in Normandy on the great D-Day invasion of Europe by U.S. and other Allied forces.

Only a few years later, in 1950, the Michigan National Guard sent the first American unit into action in the Korean War.

Michigan has been a divided state. The upper and lower parts of Michigan are split by the Straits of Mackinac, connecting Lakes Huron and Michigan. This has been good for water transportation between the two lakes, but has made it difficult to get from one part of the state to the other.

Of course, there were ferries to carry people and cars across the straits, and many tourists enjoyed the trip by ferry. But on busy days, it was sometimes necessary to wait in line for hours to get on board a ferry for the trip between the two peninsulas of Michigan.

For years people had dreamed of linking these peninsulas with a

bridge, but the distance was so great, the straits were so deep, and currents of water and wind were so strong that most plans for bridges seemed too difficult and expensive.

Then at last suitable plans were made, the builders got the go-ahead, and a really wonderful structure was completed in 1957. Someone said, "The North and the South of the state have long been engaged. Now they had a wedding ring." At the dedication of the Bridge, Governor G. Mennen Williams called it "Another Northwest Passage."

"Big Mac" as the bridge is known to almost everyone, had cost one hundred million dollars. Its distance of 8,614 feet between cable anchorages is the longest of any suspension bridge in the world. It has become one of the great tourist attractions of Michigan.

In recent years Michigan has kept pace with the modern scientific developments. There is in Michigan the largest direct single cycle boiling-water reactor in the world, for the production of atomic energy, and a Chrysler-made Jupiter C Rocket put America's very first space satellite, Explorer I, into orbit.

Collecting Your Thoughts

Were there other groups of settlers in Michigan besides the Dutch at Holland and the Mormons on Beaver Island?

How many towns have been the capital of Michigan or Michigan Territory?

Name several of Michigan's most important contributions to various wars.

Who were some of Michigan's outstanding governors?

What activities in Michigan since the Civil War interest you most?

Natural Treasures of Michigan

Michigan has received many gifts from nature. Some could easily be seen even by the first explorers—forests, fresh water, and valuable fur animals.

The great forests of Michigan covered most of the state. Even today, almost twenty million acres of land in Michigan are covered with trees. This is still over half of the state's land area. Much of the state is being reforested. Twenty million seedling pines are planted each year in Michigan.

There are eighty-five varieties of trees in Michigan—more than in any other state and more than in all of Europe. Michigan has many of the largest trees of various kinds to be found anywhere in the country. Near Ironwood, a white pine almost eighteen feet in circumference is found. A black walnut near New Haven is twelve feet eight inches in circumference, and there are many other trees of record size in Michigan.

Copper was another of Michigan's natural treasures that the early white men in Michigan saw in a few areas. Some wonderful pieces of copper were found right on the surface of the ground. The most famous of these was a huge copper boulder, larger than any ever seen before.

Many Indians and several white men had seen this valuable rock. In 1843 Julius Eldred went up the Ontonagon River, where the copper boulder was. He had to use a block and tackle and build a small railroad to the river to get the boulder out, but he was sure people would pay money to see this famous rock, and he eventually moved the metal lump to Detroit, where he put it on exhibition.

There the United States government seized it, although Eldred was supposed to have had government permission to take it. The United States officials took it to Washington, D. C., where it can still be seen in the Natural History Building of the National Museum.

The publicity about the Ontonagon Boulder interested many people in the possibilities of copper mining in Michigan.

Today, copper is still important in Michigan. The deposits of copper are among the most important anywhere. The body of copper ore in the White Pine region is supposed to be the largest known copper reserve in America.

Michigan has more than 220,000,000 tons of coal and a billion tons of peat in its reserves.

There are very large reserves of thorium available, if that metal ever becomes important in the production of atomic energy.

Great quantities of iron ore have been found in Michigan. The highest quality iron ore has already been mined. The iron that is left in Michigan is generally of lower quality. Much of this cannot be mined profitably at the present time, but new methods of preparing the ore and future needs for more ore may some day make possible greater use of Michigan's remaining supplies of iron ore.

The state has been famous for many of its birds. The very rare Kirtland, or Jack Pine warbler, is still to be found around Mio.

But one of the most famous of all birds will never be seen again. The passenger pigeon was a beautiful bird, fifteen inches long. The passenger pigeon came to Michigan early in March from its winter quarters. At one time there were probably more passenger pigeons than any other bird. It was almost impossible to describe the great flights of these birds. They flew so close together they darkened the sky. It sometimes took hours for a single flock to pass over a given spot, flying so close together that they blocked out the sun.

Commercial hunters and so-called "sportsmen" killed them by the millions. A live pigeon was tied to a stool, and when the stool was moved the bird would flap and attract hundreds of other birds to be killed. This was the beginning of our term "stool pigeon."

One of the largest gatherings of passenger pigeons on record took place near Petoskey, Michigan, in March, 1878. The beech nut trees where they roosted where weighted down so heavily with birds that branches thoughout the woods could be heard snapping off under the weight. More than a million pigeons were killed or captured at that time and place.

Forty years later there was not a single passenger pigeon in existence. Every one of the millions had been killed. The bird was extinct.

Because they are now carefully protected, the game birds that survived, such as the quail, ruffed grouse, and prairie chicken, are still to be found. Huron County claims to have the finest pheasant hunting in America, although pheasants are not native to the United States.

Michigan has also long been noted for the many varieties of fish in both its rivers and lakes, as well as in the Great Lakes.

One of Michigan's most famous and beautiful fish, the grayling trout, was caught in such quantities that it, too, became extinct in the 1930's.

Now, however, Michigan has one of the most successful and complete programs for the protection of its valuable plants and wildlife. In 1881 Michigan was the first state to provide for a paid state game warden.

Due to its wonderful forests, Michigan has had a fine variety of animals. One of the state's nicknames is the "Wolverine State." In spite of this nickname, if there were wolverine in the state they must have been there in very small numbers.

The happy otter, the opossum, black bear, raccoon, weasel, mink, skunk, badger, coyote, timber wolf, red fox, bobcat, woodchuck, beaver, muskrat, porcupine, deer, and rabbit are, or have been found in Michigan. Moose and elk were once found in the state in considerable number. The marten, woodland caribou, cougar, and bison have left the state, according to most experts.

One interesting story about animals in Michigan took place in 1912. In that year for the first time, Lake Superior froze over so solidly that moose, and possibly wolves, crossed the ice from the mainland to Isle Royale in the middle of the lake, where they had not been known before.

Collecting Your Thoughts

Explain what is meant by conservation of natural resources and tell why it is important.

What do you think are three of the most important natural resources of Michigan? Why do you choose these?

The People Use Their Treasures

Fortunes in Furs

Before the white man came to Michigan, there was some trade and manufacturing. The Indians fashioned their bark canoes, which have been called "the most perfect vehicle of their kind." Indian canoes would carry thirty times their own weight even in shallow water. The Indians also made their own snowshoes, rough clothing, and simple tools and implements. They grew some crops and evaporated the salt from salt springs.

When the white man first came, he was most interested in the beaver. Skins of these animals were much in demand in Europe. For most of the earlier years of Michigan history, the fur trade was about the only commerce in the state. Beaver skins were so valuable that they sometimes were used for money.

So many beavers were caught and killed that of course they became scarce. In 1920 there were so few beaver left that hunting or trapping them was forbidden. By 1934, the beaver population had increased enough to permit some beaver to be taken, and this has been continued.

In Michigan today there are about 7,000 licensed trappers, and the income from furs supplied by these trappers is about $750,000 per year.

The "Water Wonderland" of Michigan also provides another source of wealth. Twenty-five million pounds of fish are pulled from the sparkling waters of Michigan each year by commercial fishermen. This is in addition to all the fishing done by sportsmen.

Fortunes in Trees

The next of Michigan's treasures to receive attention was the wonderful forests. The enormous woodlands covered with the finest white pines and other trees were among the most magnificent gifts nature ever gave to mankind.

Rolland H. Maybee describes these pine lands in his book "Michigan's White Pine Era." "On the uplands and ridges were often found large, compact tracts and smaller clumps of huge monarch-like white pine. These were cloud-sweeping giants fully 125 to 170 feet tall, with large bodied trunks two to five feet in diameter at the butt, of dark gray, deeply furrowed bark.

"These straight, mammoth pines with only slight taper, towered three-quarters of their total height, clean and clear without knots, to the spreading canopy of branches and foliage of dark green, short feathery-clustered needles."

A growing America needed lumber, and so all kinds of people went to the Michigan forests hoping to make their fortunes. In the years between 1840 and 1900, the unbelievable total of 160 billion board feet came out of Michigan's standing pine timber. This was enough lumber to make ten million six-room houses. Another fifty billion board feet were cut from Michigan's cedar, hemlock, and hardwood treasures during the same period.

The lumber cut in Michigan during that sixty-year period was enough to cover the whole state with a floor one inch thick, adding the area of Rhode Island for good measure.

Michigan trees came to be called "Green Gold." Even at a low estimate the green gold of Michigan was worth far more than the yellow gold of California, which caused the gold rush in 1849. At least a billion dollars more came from the Michigan lumber than from the California gold. In the period from 1840 to 1900, the value of Michigan's lumber has been placed at two billion two hundred and twenty-five million dollars.

The Michigan lumber camps and the strong-willed men who worked them became famous, and the tales of the camps have added a complete new section to our national folklore. Everyone knows the stories of the giant imaginary lumberman, Paul Bunyan, and his blue ox, Babe, who first came to be imagined as doing their fanciful work in Michigan.

During the logging season, the rivers of the state were clogged with giant trunks being floated down to the sawmills. These lumber drives have taken a romantic place in history.

By 1873 there were more than sixteen hundred sawmills in the state of Michigan alone. Some of these mills were able to produce more than fifty million board feet per year. Lumber towns grew large and prosperous. Saginaw was once called the "Timber Capital of the World."

Several Michigan men grew so wealthy and powerful in the lumber business they came to be known as "Lumber Barons." They competed desperately to get control of the best timber lands.

By 1900 most of the best white pine forests had been destroyed completely. Desolate acres were covered with stumps or burned-over blackness, or barren sand wastes.

Many lumbermen moved on to other states. Once prosperous towns were deserted and became ghost towns. When farmers tried to use the land, they found that much of it was not suitable for farming.

Since that unfortunate period, however, Michigan has accomplished much in restoring its forest lands and building and preserving its remaining timber tracts. Lumbering is still an important industry, worth sixty million dollars a year to the state. There are still more than 400 saw, paper, pulp, and veneer mills in Michigan, most of them in the Upper Peninsula. Almost twenty million acres in Michigan remain forested. There are twenty-three state forests and five national forests in Michigan today.

Most of the world's supply of birdseye maple comes from Michigan. One hundred thousand feet of this beautiful wood were used in decorating the liner Queen Mary when it was built in 1936.

Fortunes in the Ground

The state geologist, Dr. Douglass Houghton, was the first man to discover the mineral wealth of Michigan. In 1843 there was a great mining rush. The town of Houghton, named for Michigan's great geologist, became America's first "Mining Capital." In the period between 1847 and 1887, Michigan was the leading producer of copper in the United States. Important copper deposits are still being worked.

One of the first leaders in iron mining was John Wood. He became known as "Iron" and this nickname added to his own name of Wood gave the city of "Ironwood" its name.

Today, the Mather Mine is one of the world's largest underground mines. The city of Escanaba is the only ore shipping point on Lake Michigan.

Mining in Michigan is still a four hundred million dollar a year industry.

Michigan also refined and used much of its own iron ore. In 1864, for the first time in America, steel ingots were made by the Bessemer process at the Eureka Iron Works of Eber Brock Ward in Wyandotte. In 1885, the first steel rails made in the United States were produced at Ironwood, Michigan.

One of the earliest of all mineral industries is still an important one in Michigan. The state is the country's largest producer of saline materials. Twenty-nine per cent of all the nation's salt deposits are found in the state. The sixty miles of tunnels in the International Salt Company's mines would hold the entire population of Detroit.

Manistee is one of the world's largest producers of salt, and the Dow Chemical Company at Midland, Michigan, is one of the world's largest chemical companies. It depends on the salt brines and related basic chemicals found in its region.

Gas and oil had been discovered near Howell by 1834, but it was not until the 1920's that oil and gas became important in Michigan. Today there are almost 4,000 wells producing oil or gas in the state. Carefully regulated, oil will continue to be a source of wealth for the people of Michigan for many years to come.

The Soil Brings Forth

Although it is not among the leading five states in agriculture, Michigan ranks high in many crops, especially a number of unusual crops which are not grown in very many other states.

Michigan is the largest producer of mint in the United States. The peppermint industry is centered around St. Johns. Mint is cut like hay, left for thirty-six hours to cure in the sun and then is hauled to the still where the fragrant mint oil is taken from the leaves. In addition to peppermint, spearmint is an important mint crop in Michigan.

Most of the navy beans grown in the United States are produced in Michigan's rustling bean fields. As much as 96 per cent of all the country's navy beans are produced within the state. In tribute to the beans of Michigan, in 1904 the Speaker of the United States House of Representatives, Joseph Cannon, put through a bill to serve navy bean soup every day in the Capitol restaurant. From that time, bean soup has been served there every day.

Half of all the sour cherries in the United States are produced in Michigan. Traverse City is probably the largest cherry marketing center in the United States. Most of this industry started from one orchard planted in the 1880's.

The state is also first in the growing of cucumbers and blueberries; second in strawberries, plums, and asparagus for processing. Michigan ranks third in its crops of apples, pears, grapes, and celery. Kalamazoo is sometimes called the "Celery City," and the city is known as the birthplace of America's celery production.

Benton Harbor has the world's largest non-citrus fruit and vegetable market.

The state produces more seedling evergreens than any other.

Wheat, hay, oats, turkeys, hogs, and beef cattle to the value of eighty-eight million dollars a year, are other important products of Michigan farms. In spite of all the state's water surroundings, there are 2,000 irrigated farms in Michigan. The "Thumb" country is an especially rich farming region.

Altogether, the state ranks fifteenth among all the states in agriculture.

Manufacturing Magic

Everyone connects Michigan with at least three outstanding products—automobiles, breakfast food, and furniture.

In 1836 William Haldane arrived in Grand Rapids. Mr. Haldane was a first-rate cabinet maker. He was the first in the city's long line of famous furniture makers. Many Haldane chairs of black walnut are still in use today.

The wonderful hardwoods of Michigan are particularly suitable for furniture making. By 1876 furniture making in Grand Rapids was so advanced that the manufacturers from that city showed their furniture at the Centennial exposition in Philadelphia. The response to their exhibit was so great that they could not keep up with their orders.

Since that time the name Grand Rapids has meant "furniture" in the minds of most people.

Another Michigan town has come to be associated with a particular product. The name Battle Creek is linked with cereal.

Two unusual men, Will Keith Kellogg and C. W. Post, were pioneers in the manufacture of processed breakfast foods. Today the Kellogg plant and the Post plant are the largest of their type anywhere.

Through the funds of the Kellogg Foundation, established by Mr. Kellogg, many worthwhile causes in the arts, literature, and education have received much-needed help.

When Horsepower Replaced Horses

The other city of Michigan with a name associated with a particular industry, of course, is Detroit. That city "remade America with the automobile," according to Raymond C. Miller, "and then remade the world with the techniques they have learned in the automobile plants."

First self-propelled vehicle in Michigan was probably the steam-driven car of John and Thomas Clegg, built in their machine shop at Memphis in the winter of 1884-1885. R. E. Olds built a three-wheel steam car in 1887 and drove it around Lansing.

A gasoline engine car seen on the streets of Detroit in 1896 was built by Charles G. King.

The Detroit News-Tribune of February 4, 1900, featured an article called, "Thrilling Trip on the First Detroit-Made Automobile." This was the car built by a then almost unknown young man named Henry Ford for the new Detroit Automobile Company, for which Ford was Chief Engineer.

The writer of the article said, "Looking over the latest Detroit automobile, a good impression was created. Smooth covered, box-topped, with black enameled sides, red wheels and running gear, nothing but the absence of the proverbial horse revealed the motive power was to come from within . . .

"Beyond all doubt, the automobileer—is that the new word?—will be the most important manager this coming century. He sits on a little seat, in front; and by pulling a lever and by pressing a small button in the floor, with his foot, he controls the thing with all the confidence imaginable.

"The machine runs, stops and backs at his will. He turns sharp curves with the grace and ease of a wild bird under full sail."

At this time, Michigan was mostly a rural state, with only a few people interested in the horseless carriage. One might wonder why it eventually became the world's leading automobile area.

Detroit was one of the leaders of the carriage business, so there was a background industry for the new automobile trade, but it is probably the leadership of the Detroit automobile pioneers that put the city on the road to automobile greatness.

Someone has said, "It was Ford, King and Olds who unlocked the gate to opportunity and jumped through."

The fact that the state quickly became a leader in mass production was also very important. Ransom E. Olds was a pioneer in auto mass production. In 1904 he turned out 5,000 of his "Oldsmobiles" at his new plant in Lansing. Later he formed the REO Company, using the initials of his name for the name of his new car, the Reo.

Henry Ford was associated with three companies before he became successful with his Ford Motor Company.

The year 1908 was probably the most important in the history of the automobile. In that year Ford brought out his Model T, and in that same year the General Motors Corporation, now the world's largest manufacturing organization, was formed at Detroit.

Over the years Detroit has been home to more than 170 major auto manufacturers, producing cars mostly bearing the names of the founders of the companies. Most of these names are gone from the streets today, although some like Ford, Chevrolet, Oldsmobile, Buick, and Dodge are still leaders.

Ford and his Model T kept the auto leadership for many years. Then the Model T became out of date and began to lose out to its competition, particularly Chevrolet. So Ford brought out his Model A, and finally the V-8. The Rouge plant of Ford at Dearborn is the largest industrial unit in the world not under government ownership.

It was not until 1925 that the last of the "Big Three" automobile companies came into being. In that year Walter P. Chrysler, who had been with General Motors, set up his own company. Not very much later he also took control of the very successful Dodge company, after the death of the Dodge Brothers who had founded the company.

As the home of the "Big Three," Michigan produces more motor vehicles than any other place in the world. Eighty-five per cent of all cars, trucks, and other automotive vehicles made in the United States are produced by Michigan-based companies.

Flint, Michigan's second largest city, is also second in automobile manufacture, with its Buick and Chevrolet plants, two Fisher body plants, and the A. C. Spark Plug factory. Lansing is another leading auto city, being the home of the Oldsmobile Division of General Motors, the White Motor Company, and the headquarters of the Fisher Body Division of General Motors.

In addition to motor vehicles, Michigan leads all other states in manufacture of automobile parts, trailers, boats, engines, refrigerators and office equipment. The stove and furnace industry is also one of the important manufacturing interests of the state.

The world's largest cement plant is at Alpena; Grindstone City, which still produces grindstones, once held a near monopoly on the making of grindstones. The world's largest limestone quarry is at

Presque Isle, and the Bear Archery Company is the world's largest manufacturer of archery products.

Because so much of all the magicians' equipment is manufactured at Colon, that city has come to be known as the "Magic Capital of the World."

Michigan produces more aspirin than any other area in the United States, and the first and largest canner of baby foods is the Gerber Company at Fremont. The Bissel factory at Grand Rapids is the largest manufacturer of carpet sweepers.

More recently Michigan factories have entered the space age with the manufacture of Redstone boosters and Jupiter missiles at Chrysler's near Detroit, guided missile destroyers of Defoe Ship Company at Bay City, and other computer and avionic products.

Altogether more than 2,200 manufactured products bear the label "Made in Michigan."

The Better to Travel

With its interest in automobiles, it is natural that Michigan has been a pioneer in building roads. In the early days it led in plank roads, and the world's first concrete road was laid at Detroit in 1909. Today the state's network of highways and superhighways is one of the nation's finest. Almost all of the super highways of Michigan are free of any toll.

The first transportation routes of the state, the waterways, have kept pace with the roads. The Detroit River is the busiest waterway in the world. It carries more tonnage than any other shipping lane.

Opening of the St. Lawrence Seaway in 1959 brought Detroit and all the Great Lakes ports of Michigan within reach of most of the world's ocean-going freighters. Forty lake ports of Michigan are served by freighters and passenger ships. Nineteen of its ports handle more than a million tons of freight each year. This is more million-ton ports than those of any other state. The Port of Detroit is often second only to New York City in tonnage.

On all of the upper Great Lakes there was only one closed door. Lake Superior is twenty-two feet higher than the other Great Lakes. The rapids of the St. Marys River, where the Pageant of the Soo took place in olden times, carry the waters of the river down from the level of Lake Superior. No ship could go up those rocky rapids, and only canoes and kayaks can shoot down them. Early white visitors would watch the excitement of the Indians shooting the rapids of the Soo in their frail canoes.

There was only one thing to do to get from the other lakes to the level of Lake Superior—portage your boat and all its cargo around to the up side of the rapids.

Some large ships were hauled over the portage on rollers. It took the schooner *Algonquin* a good part of the winter of 1839-1840 to move slowly upstream on the land, around the rapids. The steamboats *Independence* and *Julia Palmer* made the difficult haul in 1846. Some fair-sized boats had been built on Lake Superior and for a time this was all that was needed.

In 1850 a horse-drawn tramway began to carry cargo around the Soo rapids.

Then with the rapid growth of the mining around Lake Superior, it was apparent that a canal and locks were needed. Surprisingly enough,

there had been a canal with a lock, built on the Canadian side in 1797. This was big enough for canoes and small boats, towed by oxen, but the canal and lock had been destroyed by the Americans during the War of 1812.

To most people, building a tremendous engineering work in the middle of a wilderness seemed ridiculous, but some members of the Michigan legislature and some members of the United States Congress were far in advance of their day, and plans for a canal and locks were approved. Another man of vision was Charles T. Harvey, an agent for the Fairbanks Scale Company. His company, on his advice, took the contract to build the canal and locks. In spite of great difficulties, Harvey finished the canal and locks on schedule, in 1855.

The canal was just over a mile long and 100 feet wide. Two locks, 350 feet long and 70 feet wide, lay side by side. They were capable of raising and lowering ships eighteen feet. The cost of the canal was just under a million dollars.

At last, trade could be carried entirely by water from the farthest reaches of the Great Lakes even to the Atlantic Ocean, using the Erie Canal. The steamer Illinois was the first to pass through the locks, traveling westward. Later the same day the steamer Baltimore made the passage down to Lake Huron.

Over the years, more locks were built and older locks replaced. Today there are four American locks and one Canadian. Some of the freighters handled are more than 700 feet long.

The Soo Canal today is by far the busiest canal in the world. This waterway is probably more responsible than anything else for the fact that in the late 1800's the United States became the greatest manufacturing nation in the world and has remained so ever since.

Around the Great Lakes are all the basic raw materials needed by great industries: iron ore, coal, limestone, copper, and many others. Using the Soo Canal, all of these materials can be brought together by ship in great quantities at low cost for processing. Nowhere else in the world is this possible in just the same way or on so great a scale. Even Charles Harvey might have been somewhat surprised at the results of his vision in pushing through a canal in the wilderness.

Today, the canal and locks are among the great tourist attractions of the world.

Michigan has been a leader in other forms of transportation and communication. Its first railroad, the Erie and Kalamazoo, began operating between Adrian, Michigan, and Toledo, Ohio, in 1836.

The nation's first regularly scheduled passenger air service has already been noted as a transportation "first."

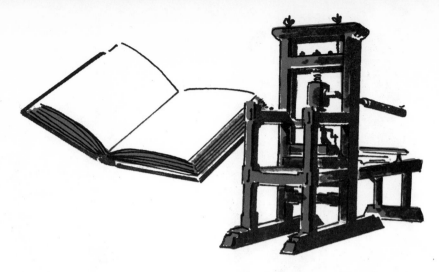

The first book printed in the whole Northwest Territory was published in Detroit in 1809, by the press established by Father Gabriel Richard. This press printed fifty-two books during its existence. The first successful newspaper in Michigan, the Detroit Gazette, was published from 1817 until 1830.

Detroit was also a leader in early radio broadcasting. Station WWJ produced the first news broadcast in history on August 31, 1920. This station also was responsible for the first broadcast of singing, the first church services on the air, and the first dance band to be heard on radio—Fred Waring and his Pennsylvanians.

So Much to See and Do

Another important industry in Michigan is based on the interesting things to see and do in the state. The tourist business in the state brings in more than $650,000,000 annually. Michigan ranks fourth among the states in total tourist, resort, and travel income.

Collecting Your Thoughts

How does the thoughtless use of our natural resources affect all of us?

Trace the important developments of water transportation in Michigan.

Find out the rank of Michigan in manufacturing among the states, of Detroit among the cities.

Why do you suppose Michigan grows so many "specialty" crops such as cherries and mint?

ANTOINE
DE LA MOTHE
CADILLAC

HENRY
FORD

Human Treasures

There are many people associated with Michigan whose names are known throughout the world, while others who may have made even more important contributions to the state may be very little known outside of Michigan.

One of the latter is Father Gabriel Richard. From the time he first was assigned to Detroit in 1798 until his death, Father Richard took a leading part in almost every worthwhile activity of his adopted town, in addition to ministering attentively to the needs of his parish.

His Bishop wrote of Father Richard: "He has a talent of doing, almost at the same time, ten things entirely different. In charge of the newspaper, aware of all political news, always ready to discuss religion when the opportunity offers and very well equipped in theology, he makes hay, gathers the fruits of his garden, picks up a peach on the ground before him, teaches one young fellow mathematics, shows another how to read, says a prayer, establishes a printing press, confesses everybody, brings over carding machines, a spinning jenny and looms to teach his parishioners how to work them, keeps his records up-to-date, demonstrates an electrical machine, visits the sick at a great distance, writes and receives letters from everywhere, preaches every Sunday and feast day, at length and wisely, adds to his library, spends the nights without sleep, is on the go all day long, loves to talk, sees company, catechises his young parishioners, looks after a school for girls, carries himself well, as well physically at the age of fifty as most men are at thirty. . . ."

LEWIS CASS

FATHER
RICHARD

GENERAL CUSTER

THOMAS DEWEY

RALPH BUNCHE

In one of his many efforts to aid education, Father Richard was helpful in preparing the way for the founding of the University of Michigan.

In 1823 Father Richard was elected the representative of Michigan territory in the Congress at Washington. He was the only Catholic priest who has ever been a member of Congress.

He printed the first book in Michigan and published the first newspaper. He held services for the Protestants of the area until a Protestant minister came.

During the War of 1812, the British arrested Father Richard. It is interesting to note that the British freed him at the request of their ally, the great Indian Chief Tecumseh.

Father Richard, as someone has said, "was, in his humble way, an empire builder." Others have called Father Gabriel Richard "The Patron Saint of Detroit."

Another priest, who spent much of his life in the wilds of the Upper Peninsula, was Father Frederic Baraja. During his many years of missionary work with the Indians he translated a hymn book into the Chippewa language and compiled a Chippewa dictionary. He was called "The Parish Priest of Lake Superior." Finally he was made bishop of the region, with headquarters at Sault Ste. Marie, and later at Marquette.

Public Figures

The second governor of Michigan Territory, Lewis Cass, was also a young man, although not as young as Governor Stevens, who later became first governor of Michigan as a state. Governor Cass was only thirty-one when he became the chief executive of Michigan Territory. He served for eighteen years in that post, later served the nation as United States Senator, as United States Secretary of War, and Minister to France. He became a candidate for President, but was defeated by Zachary Taylor, in 1848. Lewis Cass has been called "Michigan's foremost historic citizen."

Another Michigan man who was twice a candidate for the office of

President of the United States was Thomas E. Dewey, born in Owosso. He gained his early fame in New York, where he became a prominent governor of that state. As Republican candidate, he was defeated in the race for President by Franklin D. Roosevelt and later by Harry Truman.

Ralph J. Bunche, born in Detroit, received the Nobel Peace prize in 1950 for his work as an officer of the United Nations.

A Dashing General

One of Michigan's most prominent military men was General George Armstrong Custer, who became a national hero during the Civil War. He was made a general at the amazingly early age of twenty-three. He and his men are generally credited with helping to turn the tide of battle at Gettysburg.

Later, of course, as the commander of U.S. Indian fighters, General Custer became the central figure in what we call "Custer's last stand," where he and 225 of his men were killed on the desolate banks of the Little Big Horn River in Montana. Not a man was spared, and the dead included Custer's two brothers, his nephew and a brother-in-law. Today a national cemetery covers with green the area where the slopes flowed red with blood in 1876.

This was a dramatic end to a notable military record. Sadly, however, military authorities today hold Custer responsible for the tragedy and say that it probably could have been avoided with the proper action on the general's part.

Merchant Princes

Several merchandising giants have been associated with Michigan. Sebastian S. Kresge of Detroit founded the great Kresge variety store chain. The originator of the modern mail order business, Montgomery Ward, grew up in Niles, Michigan. Harry Gordon Selfridge, who established the most famous department store in London, Selfridge's, came from Jackson, Michigan. J. L. Hudson of Detroit was another of the state's merchandising magnates.

DETROIT

Four Wheels and an Engine

Of all the men who made Michigan famous through the development of the automobile, Henry Ford is probably the most prominent. He has been called "the man who most influenced the tide of world economy during the 20th century."

Ford "revolutionized industry with three concepts." He created the modern production line. He was the first to see that if he made a product that enough people wanted to have and could afford to buy there would be created what we call a "mass market," and he was the first to see that a liberal wage policy for his employees was good business as well as fair labor policy.

In January, 1914, Ford announced that he would pay his workers five dollars for an eight hour work day. This was such an unbelievably high wage for those days that his competitors felt he probably would go bankrupt. So many workers came to apply for jobs that there were riots on Woodward Avenue, across from the plant.

Instead of going bankrupt the Ford business prospered. The methods of production that he and his associates developed were responsible for the ability of the Ford plant to pay higher wages and still earn a profit. The moving assembly line made it possible to produce a Ford every six hours in 1914. Less than a year before the new assembly lines were started almost ten hours were required to produce a new Ford.

Although they are not generally given the credit, Henry Ford and his son Edsel Ford, along with William B. Stout, were probably more responsible for the success of commercial aviation than any other individuals.

Mr. Ford hated war, and in 1914 he called a mediation conference and sent what was called the "Ford Peace Ship," which sailed from New York with the hope of bringing about peace but with no very clear idea of how this could be done. When the ship and its passengers returned in 1916, they had talked with many prominent people on both sides of the war and had held many peace meetings, but peace was as far away as ever.

Henry Ford never gave up his ideas of trying to make the world a better place. With Edsel Ford he established the Ford Foundation. With its many hundreds of millions of dollars, this is the largest of all the foundations. Through his foundation, Mr. Ford's ideas of helping education and culture and of promoting better government and public affairs are constantly being promoted, many years after his death.

Unusual Accomplishments

An accidental gunshot wound on Mackinac Island was the strange beginning of one of the most famous scientific studies of all time. A young trapper, Alexis St. Martin, was severely wounded in the abdomen by the shot, and the wound never healed, although St. Martin recovered and seemed perfectly healthy otherwise.

A physician on the island, Dr. William Beaumont, began to study the opening in St. Martin's stomach. For the first time it was possible to observe the processes of digestion. He became known as the man with a "window in his stomach." Dr. Beaumont's reports on these observations offered great advances in our knowledge of digestive processes and made him world famous. They hold good even today, almost 150 years after St. Martin's accident.

St. Martin, who lived an almost normal life in spite of his difficulties, married, reared a family and lived to be eighty.

Another Michigan man who became famous for an unusual accomplishment was Charles A. Lindbergh, who was born in Detroit. When he flew his plane the "Spirit of St. Louis" from New York to Paris in the first solo flight across the Atlantic, it seemed that the world had never seen such excitement. The "Lone Eagle," as Lindbergh came to be called, was hailed everywhere as one of the great heroes of all time.

The prominence that Lindbergh's flight gave to aviation was another extremely important cause of the rapid rise of commercial flying.

The great inventor Thomas A. Edison spent part of his boyhood at Port Huron and invented an electric battery there. One of the world's most influential labor leaders, Walter Reuther, is a Michigan man, and the famous atomic scientist and Nobel Prize winner, Glenn T. Seaborg, comes from Ishpeming.

Words, and Words with Music

Many prominent writers and song writers have been associated with Michigan. One of the world's most popular poets was Edgar A. Guest of Detroit. Will Carleton based his famous "Over the Hills to the Poorhouse" at Hillsdale. He practiced his well-known lectures on his farm animals and said the horses generally went to sleep during the lectures.

Another famous Hillsdale landmark is the bell that hangs in the village square. This is the bell written about in Rose Hartwick Thorpe's "Curfew Shall Not Ring Tonight."

Still another well-loved writer was Edna Ferber of Kalamazoo.

One of the best liked of all hymns, "The Old Rugged Cross," was composed at Albion by the Reverend George Bennard, a Methodist minister. At his home on U.S. 131 near Reed City there is now a large wooden cross to mark the spot. A three-ton granite cross at Pokagon marks the site where the song was sung for the first time.

A prominent composer of popular tunes, Dick Whiting, made his headquarters in Detroit. He sold his first song, "Kiss Your Baby Good-bye," when he was only seventeen. His later hits included many works familiar to almost everyone, such as: "Till We Meet Again," "Japanese Sandman," "Louise," "My Ideal," "Beyond the Blue Horizon," and the "Good Ship Lollipop."

Although the poet Henry Wadsworth Longfellow had no personal connection with Michigan one of his most famous poems was *Hiawatha*. This poem made its Michigan setting world famous. *Hiawatha* was based on the writings of Henry R. Schoolcraft. On his trip with Governor Cass in 1820, Schoolcraft had become extremely interested in the Indians and their culture. He married an educated woman, Jane Johnston, who was part Indian. With his wife's help, Schoolcraft gathered information on the Indians and their lives until he became one of the greatest authorities on Indians. He published many books on the Indians, and it was this material that gave Longfellow the background information for his Indian writings.

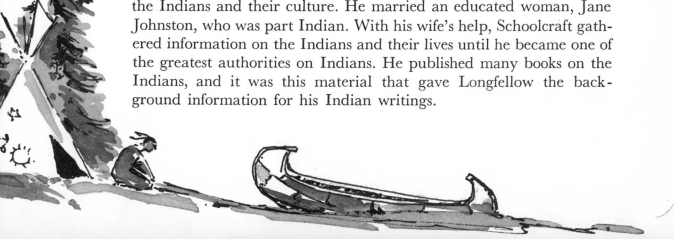

Music—In Forest and City

One of the most unusual and best-known musical organizations anywhere is the National Music Camp at Interlochen, founded by Joseph E. Maddy. This is a summer school in a beautiful woodland setting, where talented music students can learn the fine points of great music from prominent teachers and have an opportunity to play music with other young people.

This idea·of teaching music in such an outdoor setting has spread to many other parts of the country and to other countries, as well.

Another well-known Michigan musical organization is the Detroit Symphony. Founded in 1914, it came into its own with the selection of Ossip Gabrilowitsch as its permanent conductor. By the beginning of its sixth year, the orchestra had a new building for a permanent home and a regular playing membership of ninety men. William H. Murphy and Horace E. Dodge each gave $100,000 for the new building, and other subscriptions came in to make the building possible.

Collecting Your Thoughts

What Michigan men and women would you most have liked to meet? Why?

Name three fields in which Michigan people have been especially important.

Teaching and Learning

Michigan early showed its support of education by becoming the first state providing for a State Superintendent of Public Instruction.

The University of Michigan is considered the first university ever established by any of the states. It is now known as the "Mother of State Universities." It had its beginnings at Detroit as early as 1817 through the advanced thinking and efforts of such men as Lewis Cass, William Woodbridge, Judge Augustus B. Woodward, Father Gabriel Richard, and the Reverend John Monteith. Its modern history did not begin until it moved to Ann Arbor in 1837. A gift of land from the Indians to the University of Michigan at the Treaty of Fort Meigs gave great help and encouragement to the school at an early date in its development.

The first university hospital in the United States was established at the University of Michigan in 1869. It also had the first school of public health in the country.

It was the first *major* university to admit women in this country. In 1902, the University football team won the very first Rose Bowl game ever played. Michigan Stadium of the University seats 101,000 and is the largest college-owned stadium in the United States.

Michigan State University at Lansing is said to be the oldest institution in the world devoted to teaching scientific agriculture. Its first building was erected in 1857.

Wayne State University is the largest center of learning in Detroit. Michigan has six other state colleges and universities. Altogether there are seventy-four college-level institutions in Michigan.

Collecting Your Thoughts

See if you can learn how many of Michigan's colleges and universities are "accredited."

Why are colleges and universities important to a state?

Enchantment of Michigan

Detroit

Michigan is one of the most popular of all tourist states. As the oldest major city in the midwest, Detroit is one of the leading tourist attractions. Oddly enough, Detroit is the only place in the United States where you can look directly south into Canada. A glance at the map shows how this can be so.

Detroit had been a town for 125 years before it felt the need for a town hall. Today the city-county building, which was built in 1955, is part of a great new civic center, designed to be one of the finest of its kind.

Visitors to Detroit are impressed with the Veterans' Memorial Building on the site where Cadillac and his French settlers first landed in 1701. The Children's Museum, Detroit Institute of Arts, Historical Museum, and the International Institute of Folk Art, which displays exhibits of forty-three nationalities, all are attractions of Detroit.

Detroit claims to have the largest Masonic Temple in the world, and the Masonic building has an entire cathedral within its walls.

The park on Belle Isle in the Detroit River ranks high among America's city parks. It offers an aquarium, horticulture building, children's zoo, gardens, riding stables and many other attractions. The island is supposed to have taken its name from that of Governor Lewis Cass's daughter, Isabella. The English first bought it from the Indians for five barrels of rum, three rolls of tobacco, three pounds of red paint, and a belt of wampum. This amounts to about $970, which is still more than another group of Indians received for all of Manhattan Island.

The Dossin Great Lakes Museum is located on the south shore of Belle Isle. It tells the great story of ships and men on the lakes. There is a fine collection of lake ship models and Great Lakes marine paintings at the museum.

An annual attraction at Detroit is the State Fair, which is the oldest of all state fairs and was established in 1849.

Among Detroit's many memorials is a bronze statue of Stevens T. Mason, where his body was taken in 1905 from the East where he had died in a kind of self-imposed exile from his beloved Michigan. Michigan's youngest governor was only thirty-one when he died.

One of the finest residential sections in the country is Grosse Point, Detroit's exclusive residential suburb on Lake St. Clair.

Fort Wayne is another attraction for visitors at Detroit. The Fort was built in 1846 and named in honor of Mad Anthony Wayne. Fortunately, the fort can still be seen today almost exactly as it was. It is considered the best preserved pre-Civil-War fort in the United States. Exhibits inside the buildings at the fort tell the story of Detroit's progress from a small fortified trading post to its present position.

Dearborn Pushes Back the Clock

One of the most frequently visited tourist areas anywhere is Dearborn, where Henry Ford founded so many interesting museums and exhibits. Dearborn is the home of the Henry Ford Museum and Greenfield Village.

Particularly popular is the "Street of Early American Shops," showing the work of craftsmen who used hand tools. Visitors can see the work being done in those shops exactly as it must have been done in the early days. There is a candle shop, wrought iron shop, toy shop, gun and locksmith shop, millinery shop, and fancy goods shop. Also in the museum are displays of early autos, historic planes, locomotives, and other mechanical arts.

Visitors who stay at the Dearborn Inn can be accommodated for the night in the homes of famous people such as Walt Whitman, Edgar Allan Poe, Barbara Fritchie, and Oliver Wolcott. Inside, these homes have been redesigned to accommodate guests.

Ford considered Greenfield Village his tribute to American men of genius. He gave particular attention to Thomas A. Edison in the Edison Institute and Menlo Park compound.

BLACKSMITH SHOP

Visitors often ask what prompted Mr. Ford to honor Edison's memory. He is generally thought to have considered Edison the greatest American. Edison was also the first prominent person to encourage Ford in his development of the automobile. Edison's laboratory at Menlo Park, New Jersey, has been reproduced with great accuracy. Even the reddish soil around the laboratory has been imported from New Jersey.

At Greenfield Village there are more than 100 historic buildings. These have been moved there from all sections of the country and restored when necessary. They include the bicycle shop of the Wright Brothers and the birthplace of Ford himself. The visitor may ride a horse-drawn carriage, sail on a Mississippi paddlewheel steamer, view an old mill, visit a blacksmith shop or have a tintype taken.

Holland in America

In 1847 a group of Dutch settlers chose a site for a new town in Michigan and called their little settlement Holland in honor of the country of their birth. In the early years, most of the Dutch settlers who flocked to Holland were escaping from religious persecution.

WRIGHT
CYCLE SHOP

ROSE COTTAGE

The Dutch people at Holland, Michigan, were extremely hardworking and industrious. With their own labor they dug a canal to connect the town with Lake Michigan. And they even built their own bridge. Before long the new town was prospering. All through its early years the great leader of Holland was its founder, the Reverend Albertus Christiaan Van Raalte.

Today, Holland is a center of thriving businesses and industry. Among other factories, it has the only wooden shoe manufacturing plant in this country.

Holland is also the home of one of the best and most noted annual festivals in the country. This is the annual Tulip Festival. For Festival time in May the residents wear Dutch costumes and wooden shoes. There are floral parades, and pageants, and tulips everywhere. Great crowds are always attracted to Holland for the event.

More Enchantment in Southern Michigan

Several southern Michigan cities have unusual names. Two pioneer settlers in one of these towns both had wives named "Ann." These ladies liked to sit under their grape arbor so much that their husbands named the town "Ann Arbor," which today is the celebrated home of the University of Michigan.

At Ann Arbor today, of course, among the principal points of interest are the grounds, buildings, museums, and other attractions of the University.

In its Indian form, the name Kalamazoo means "where the water boils in the pot." The city was the first to build a permanent mall in the United States. This was done by taking all vehicles off the principal shopping street and turning it into a beautiful parklike area. Since Kalamazoo pioneered this plan, a number of other cities across the country have created similar malls.

When an early land surveyor and an Indian had a fight on the banks of a creek in 1825 they could hardly have known that their "battle" was going to give its name to the city of Battle Creek. Among the many attractions of Battle Creek, the Leila Arboretum is said to be

one of the finest in the world. The W. K. Kellogg Bird Sanctuary on Wintergreen Lake near Battle Creek is the largest of its kind in the country.

Visitors to the region of Bloomfield Hills may well be surprised by the music which seems to float through the air. They are listening to the world's largest carillon, installed in 1960 at the Kirk-in-the-Hills Presbyterian Church. There are seventy-seven bells, weighing a total of sixty-six tons.

Nearby Adrian is known as the "Maple City of Michigan." It was the terminal of the first railroad built west of New York State and connected Adrian with Toledo, thirty miles away.

At Lansing, the Capitol building is made of sandstone, having a rotunda paved with glass blocks set into an iron framework to form the floor. From the rotunda floor, the visitor can look up to the top of the dome, 175 feet above. There is a grand staircase on either side of the rotunda. One hundred and twenty-three battered, bullet-torn flags are displayed in cases around the rotunda. These are the Civil War battle flags of Michigan.

When the Capitol was dedicated in 1879, it was very much in advance of its time. Gas lights were instantly lit by electric switches. There was a steam-operated elevator.

Two state office buildings at Lansing have been named for early governors. These are the Lewis Cass building and the Stevens T. Mason Building.

The second largest collection of fingerprints in the United States is on file at the Michigan State Police Headquarters in East Lansing. Only the FBI file at Washington is larger, but the FBI file was established after the Michigan file, which was the model for the one in Washington.

Near Lansing, at Eaton Rapids, is the national headquarters for the Veterans of Foreign Wars organization. This is a city in itself on a 640 acre site and serves as the home for several hundred widows and orphans of veterans.

One of the unusual organizations of Michigan is the House of David, a religious group founded in 1903 at Benton Harbor by Benjamin Purnell. They are particularly remembered for their famous long-bearded baseball team.

A large furniture division of the Grand Rapids Public Museum is said to be the only one of its exact kind.

Jackson is noted for its illuminated cascades of water. A much more grim landmark of Jackson is the State Prison of Southern Michigan, thought to be the world's largest walled prison.

The Court House of Lapeer County is supposed to be the oldest in the state, where it was built in 1839.

Frankenmuth is noted for its Church Bells in the Forest and the famous chicken dinners at its three hotels.

Chesaning, not far from Saginaw, is proud to entertain visitors on its showboat.

The mysterious sinkholes of Alpena are another tourist attraction.

Across the state, at Muskegon, is the grave of Jonathan Walker, who was the "Man With the Branded Hand" in the writings of John Greenleaf Whittier. Lumber Baron Charles Hackley's contribution made possible the fine art museum at Muskegon.

Places of Enchantment in the Northern Tier

The site of Ludington is remembered as the place where the famous explorer-priest Jacques Marquette died in 1675. Father Marquette had been pushing on to reach his mission at St. Ignace where he could be treated for his serious illness, but his brave heart gave out, and his companions buried him near the spot where he died.

Father Marquette's body was moved two years after his death to St. Ignace. The town where he died was first called Marquette, but the name was later changed to the name of its founder, James Ludington.

Of course, at the time of Father Marquette's death there was no town there, but at the place where his death occurred is a memorial cross, and the river that empties into Lake Michigan very near by is called the Pere Marquette in his memory.

Bad Axe, county seat of Huron County, is another Michigan community that was named for an unusual reason.

When a surveyor found a broken axe handle, he simply called the spot Bad Axe, and that has been its name ever since.

Midland, Michigan, home of the Dow Chemical Company, claims to have more churches of modern architecture than any other city.

On the Sable River in Iosco County an attraction is the Lumberman's Memorial.

Houghton Lake, source of the Muskegan River, is the largest lake wholly inside the boundaries of Michigan.

A unique memorial is the one found at Kewadin in Antrim County. This is a cairn built of stones from all eighty-three of Michigan's counties, in memory of Hugh J. Gray, the man who founded organized tourist promotion in the state.

Frankfort has gained an international reputation as a glider-soaring site. Because the winds and other conditions there seem to be just right, many world records in gliding have been set there.

Although not many Indians remain in Michigan, the Ottawa Indians still maintain their tribal capital at Harbor Springs and hold their ceremonial assemblies there each year.

One of the great opera houses of the world was built at Manistee by lumber king T. J. Ramsdell around the turn of the last century. It was one of the largest of its time and still has one of the greatest stages anywhere. It is used now as a summer theater. The salt brine found at Manistee has been noted for its use in health bath immersion treatments. The name Manistee in the Indian language has the romantic translation of "Spirit of the Woods."

One of the Indian legends collected by Henry R. Schoolcraft tells of the mother bear and her two cubs who started to swim across Lake Michigan to look for food. Just before they reached the shore the two cubs sank. The mother bear crawled up on the shore and lay down on the bank where she could look out over the spot where her cubs drowned. Before long the shifting sands covered her. Today, the story goes, that mother bear has become Sleeping Bear sand dune, and two small islands off the shore are the bear cubs.

At any rate, Sleeping Bear dune is a very popular spot, where people of all ages love to climb or ride over the sand of the largest shifting sand dune in the world.

Another island with many memories is Beaver Island. Twenty buildings of the Mormon period have been preserved, and "King Strang's" home is now open to visitors as a museum. On the island is the grave of Dr. Fedore Protar, a Russian Count, exiled by the Czar for freeing his serfs. Dr. Protar doctored the residents of the island without ever charging them a fee.

Glen Lake is one of the most beautiful lakes anywhere.

The world's longest toboggan run at Grayling sweeps tobogganists down its 3,000 foot length at speeds up to 100 miles per hour.

Near Traverse City at the tip of Old Mission Peninsula runs an imaginary line exactly half way between the Equator and the North Pole.

On Burt Lake, near Indian River, is the Indian River Shrine. A cross thirty-one feet high bears what is thought to be the largest figure ever made to represent Christ.

Another attraction for visitors in the upper part of the Lower Peninsula is the National Music Camp at Interlochen, where many outstanding music performances are offered by the leading music students who study there during the summer and who enjoy the camp recreation and the woodland setting.

Of course, the area around Mackinaw City has some of the most interesting attractions in the state. "Big Mac," as the Mackinac Bridge is familiarly known, is one of the world's great tourist attractions in its own right, as well as being a tremendous help to traffic entering or leaving the Upper Peninsula.

Almost in the shadow of Big Mac is old Fort Michilimackinac, where restoration was begun in 1959.

Few areas in the United States have been the scene of more dramatic and historic events than Mackinac Island. The Indian name is thought to mean "Great Turtle" because of the island's shape. Almost from the very beginning of recorded history of the area, Mackinac Island has played an important part.

The island is located at the crossroads, north and south and east and west, of a very large territory. It had a long and important history even before Detroit was founded. It was often thought of as "The Key to the New World."

Now Mackinac Island is more often thought of as the "Bermuda of the North."

Today, in addition to being a pleasant summer resort, with the largest summer hotel in the world, the island has kept alive its historic memories for its visitors. The effect of the past is strengthened by the fact that no automobiles are allowed on the island, and visitors travel by carriage or bicycle.

On its high bluff overlooking the harbor, Old Fort Mackinac stands guard. Built in 1780, it is preserved as nearly as possible just as it looked then. There are many natural scenic wonders scattered about the island, such as Arch Rock. On Mackinac Island, visitors find themselves in the only place where the sun rises in one Great Lake and sets in another.

It is strange to learn that Mackinac Island had been named a national park in 1875, but was turned over to Michigan in 1895 and became Michigan's first state park.

Enchantment in the Land of Hiawatha

There still is one national park within Michigan's boundaries. That is wonderful Isle Royale National Park, where there are no roads or wheeled vehicles, and the whole area is almost unchanged by man. The nearest mainland is twenty-two miles away from this island, which is the largest in Lake Superior. It is forty-five miles long, five to eight miles wide, and is surrounded by more than 200 smaller islands.

On Isle Royale is one of the largest remaining herds of great antlered moose in the United States. They are supposed to have crossed over to the island on the ice in the severe winter of 1912. When the ice melted they could no longer get back to the mainland, but this was fortunate for them since they found protection there.

A great tourist center of the Upper Peninsula is the region of the St. Marys River, centered at Sault Ste. Marie. There is much to be seen in this oldest of all the cities in Michigan, including a Chippewa museum containing many relics of the Indian times. This is housed in the historic building where Henry Schoolcraft wrote his *Indian Tales*, from which Longfellow wrote *Hiawatha*.

In Sault Ste. Marie, visitors may also see a model of the city, the river, canal, and locks as they looked in the mid 1850's when the first locks and canal were new.

Sault Ste. Marie is the only gateway between Canada and the United States on a stretch of the border that is 300 miles long.

Skiing in the Upper Peninsula is world renowned. Ski jumping in the United States had its beginning at Ishpeming in 1887. Today the National Ski Museum and the National Ski Hall of Fame are both at Ishpeming.

Tahquamenon Falls, near Newberry, is the largest waterfall east of the Mississippi with the exception of Niagara.

Porcupine Mountains State Park in Ontonagon County is the largest recreational state park in the nation. It covers 58,000 acres. Another popular Upper Peninsula state park is Fort Wilkins State Park at Copper Harbor, with its stockade restored and maintained as a frontier post.

More Enchantment

Altogether Michigan offers fifty-eight state parks for the pleasure of its residents and visitors. There are more than 4,000 roadside picnic tables at 112 roadside parks. There are more than seventy developed ski areas—the greatest number in the country.

Collecting Your Thoughts

Suggest three reasons why Michigan is a great vacation state.
What place in Michigan would you think would be most interesting to visit? Why?

Handy Reference Section

Instant Facts

Became 26th State — January, 1837

Capital — Lansing

State Bird — Robin

State Flower — Apple Blossom

State Tree — White Pine

State Motto — Si Quaeris Peninsulam Amoename Circumspice (If you seek a pleasant peninsula, look about you)

Area — 96,791 Square Miles (including water areas)

Greatest Length (north to south) — 310 Miles

Greatest Width — (east to west) — 400 Miles

Highest Point — 1,980 Feet

Lowest Point — 572 Feet

Population — 7,823,194 (1960)

Highest Recorded Temperature — 112°

Lowest Recorded Temperature — Minus 51°

Population Density — 137.2 Persons Per Square Mile

Principal Cities —		
Detroit	1,670,144	(1960)
Flint	196,940	
Grand Rapids	177,313	
Dearborn	112,007	
Lansing	107,807	

You Have a Date with History

1622   Etienne Brule and Grenoble, first white men in Michigan

1634   Jean Nicolet passed through Straits of Mackinac

1641   Isaac Jokues and Charles Raymbault reached rapids, which they called Sault de Sainte Marie

1668	Marquette and Dablon founded first permanent settlement in Michigan at the Soo
1669	Adrien Jolliet first white man in Lower Peninsula
1671	Francois Daumont claimed interior of continent for French
1673	Marquette and Jolliet left St. Ignace on exploration
1675	Death of Father Marquette near present day Ludington
1679	La Salle built Fort Miami on site of present St. Joseph
1686	Daniel Greysolon built Fort St. Joseph at present Port Huron
1701	Cadillac founded Detroit
1760	French rule in Detroit ended
1781	Spanish flag raised over Fort St. Joseph for short time
1783	Treaty of Paris
1787	Ordinance of 1787 established Northwest Territory
1796	British evacuated Detroit
1802	Detroit incorporated as a town
1805	Michigan Territory created, Detroit as Capital
1808	American Fur Company founded by John Jacob Astor
1812	Detroit surrendered to British
1813	Detroit recaptured
1818	First steamboat at Detroit
1835	Toledo War
1837	Michigan admitted to Union
1841	University of Michigan opened at Ann Arbor
1844	Iron ore discovered at Negaunee
1848	Legislature met for first time in Capitol in Lansing
1854	Republican party organized at Jackson
1855	Sault Ste. Marie ship canal opened
1871	Forest fires
1879	New State Capitol dedicated at Lansing
1896	First automobile at Detroit
1908	First Model T Fords
1929	Ambassador Bridge opened between Detroit and Windsor
1930	Detroit-Windsor tunnel opened
1935	United Automobile Workers organized
1957	Mackinac Bridge opened

Thinkers, Doers, Fighters
Men and Women Who Helped Make Michigan Great

Baraja, Father Frederic
Beaumont, Dr. William
Bunche, Ralph J.
Cadillac, Antoine de la Mothe
Cass, Lewis
Cavelier, Robert (Sieur de la Salle)
Chrysler, Walter P.
Custer, George Armstrong
Daumont, Francois (Sieur de
  St. Lusson)
Dow, Herbert H.
Ford, Edsel
Ford, Henry
Gabrilowitsch, Ossip
Gray, Hugh J.
Guest, Edgar A.
Haldane, William
Harvey, Charles T.
Houghton, Douglass

Hudson, J. L.
Jolliet, Adrian
Jolliet, Louis
Kellogg, Will Keith
King, Charles G.
Kresge, Sebastian S.
Lindbergh, Charles A.
Marquette, Father Jacques
Mason, Steven T.
Monteith, John
Nicolet, Jean
Olds, Ransom E.
Post, C. W.
Richard, Father Gabriel
Stout, William B.
Schoolcraft, Henry
Van Raalte, Rev. Albertus
  Christiaan
Woodward, Augustus

Annual Events

January — Tipuptown Festival (Ice Fishing) Houghton Lake
February — Winter Carnival, Alpena
        — Ice Revue, Escanaba
May — National Mushroom Contest, Boyne City
    — Blossom Festival, Blessing of the Blossoms, Benton Harbor
    — Tulip Festival, Holland
June — Lilac Festival, Mackinac Island
July — Sailing Races, to Mackinac Island
    — Top O' Michigan Marathon, outboard races, Cheboygan
August — Potato Festival, Munger
September — Walking Races, International Walkers Assn., across
    Mackinac Bridge (Labor Day)
        — Archery Festival, Lewiston
October — Red Flannel Festival, Cedar Springs
        — Women's National Bear Hunt, Kalkaska
        — National Automobile Show, Detroit
November — Santa Claus Parade, Detroit

The Governors of Michigan

Steven T. Mason, 1835-1840

William Woodbridge, 1840-1841

James Wright Gordon, Lieut. Gov.,
  1841

John S. Barry, 1842-1846

Alpheus Felch, 1846-1847

William L. Greenly, Lieut. Gov., 1847

Epaphroditus Ransom, 1848-1850

John S. Barry, 1850-1851

Robert McClelland, 1852-1853

Andrew Parsons, Lieut. Gov., 1853-
  1854

Kingsley S. Bingham, 1855-1858

Moses Wisner, 1859-1860

Austin Blair, 1861-1864

Henry H. Crapo, 1865-1868

Henry P. Baldwin, 1869-1872

John J. Bagley, 1873-1876

Charles M. Croswell, 1877-1880

David H. Jerome, 1881-1882

Josiah W. Begole, 1883-1884

Russell A. Alger, 1885-1886

Cyrus G. Luce, 1887-1890

Edwin B. Winans, 1891-1892

John T. Rich, 1893-1896

Hazen S. Pingree, 1897-1900

Aaron T. Bliss, 1901-1904

Fred M. Warner, 1905-1910

Chase S. Osborn, 1911-1912

Woodbridge N. Ferris, 1913-1916

Albert E. Sleeper, 1917-1920

Alexander J. Groesbeck, 1921-1926

Fred W. Green, 1927-1930

Wilber M. Brucker, 1931-1932

William A. Comstock, 1933-1934

Frank D. Fitzgerald, 1935-1936

Frank Murphy, 1937-1938

Frank D. Fitzgerald, 1939

Luren D. Dickinson, Lieut. Gov.,
  1939-1940

Murray D. Van Wagoner, 1941-1942

Harry F. Kelly, 1943-1946

Kim Sigler, 1947-1948

G. Mennen Williams, 1949-1960

John B. Swainson, 1961-1963

George Romney, 1963-

ANGELL HALL
UNIVERSITY OF MICHIGAN

INDEX